Jesus Is Born

ISBN 0-634-03282-8

HAL•LEONARD®
CORPORATION
7777 W. BLUEMOUND RD. P.O. BOX 13819 MILWAUKEE, WI 53213

Visit Hal Leonard Online at
www.halleonard.com

CONTENTS

AFTER DECEMBER SLIPS AWAY

Words and Music by BONNIE KEEN
and LOWELL ALEXANDER

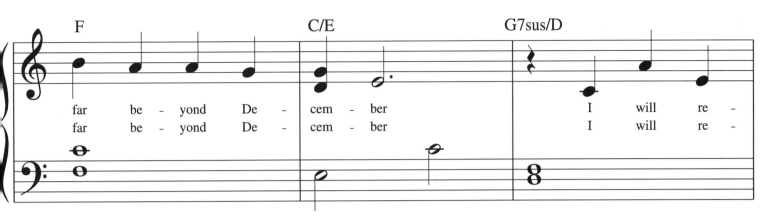

far   be - yond   De - cem - ber
far   be - yond   De - cem - ber   I   will   re -
I   will   re -

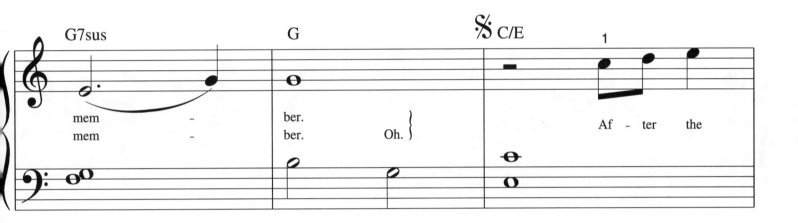

mem   -   ber.   C/E
mem   -   ber.   Oh.   Af - ter   the

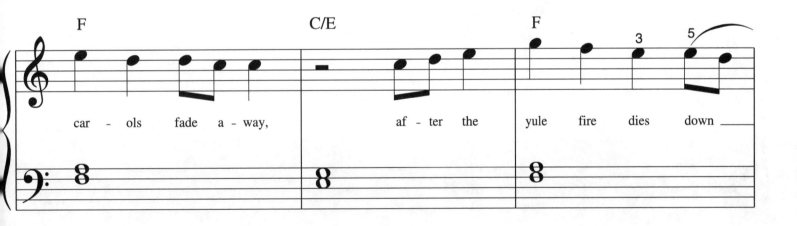

car - ols   fade a - way,   af - ter the   yule   fire   dies   down ___

___   when   there   are   no   long - er   dreams ___   to   o -   pen   and

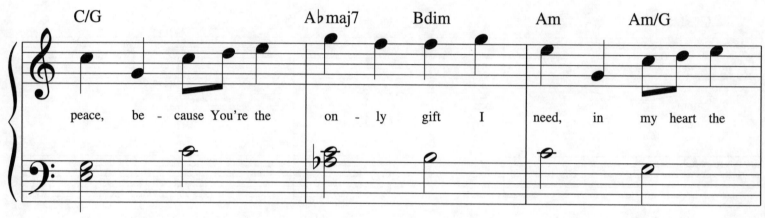

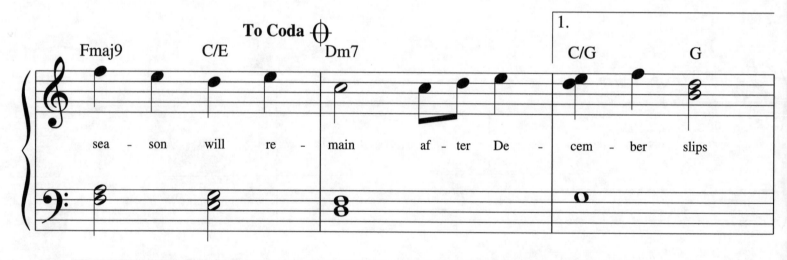

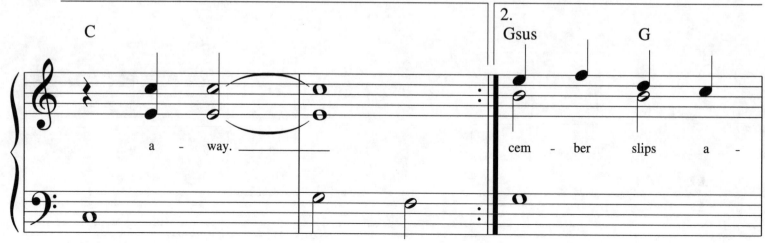

8

ALL IS WELL

Words and Music by MICHAEL W. SMITH
and WAYNE KIRKPATRICK

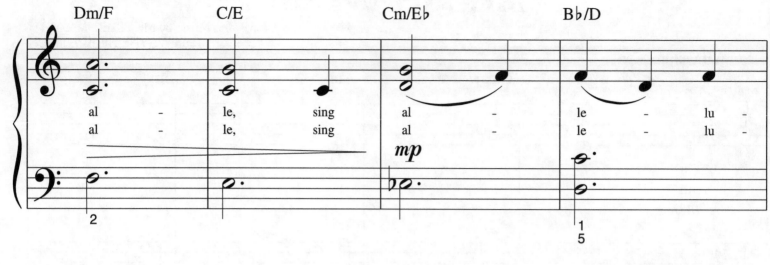

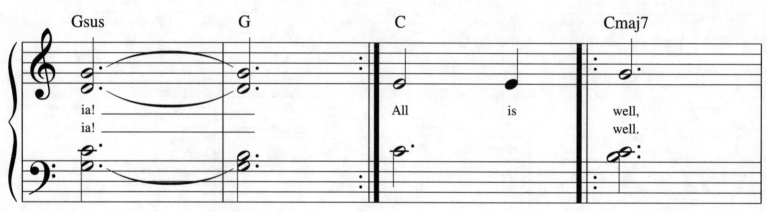

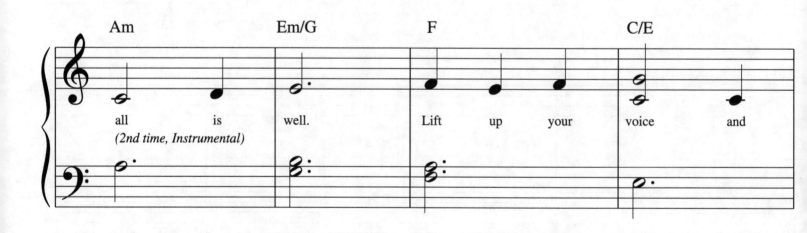

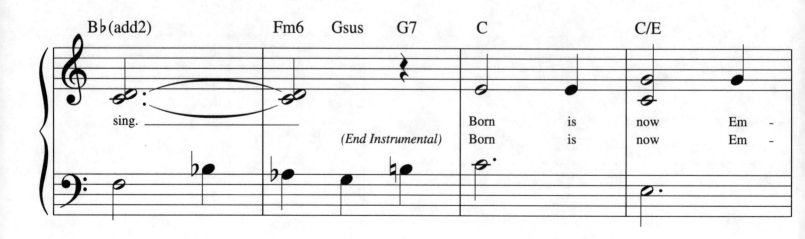

CELEBRATE THE CHILD

Words and Music by
MICHAEL CARD

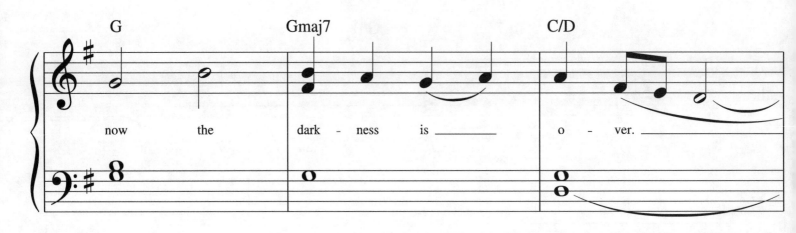

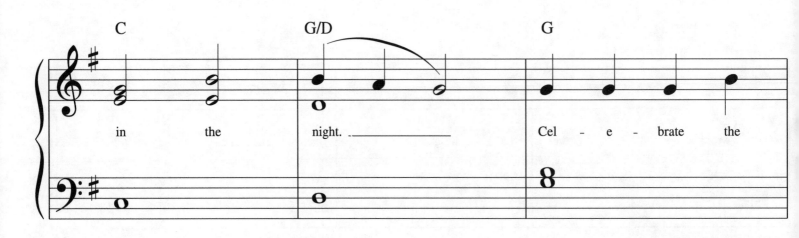

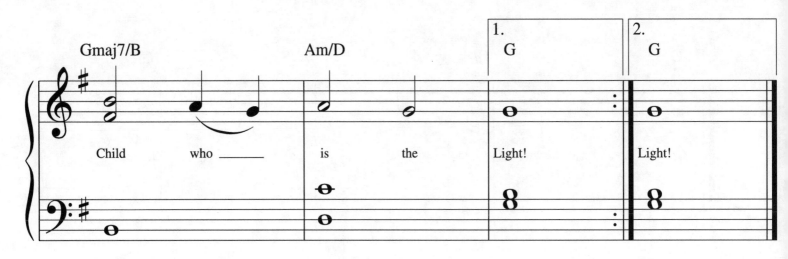

GOING HOME FOR CHRISTMAS

Words and Music by STEVEN CURTIS CHAPMAN
and JAMES ISAAC ELLIOT

18

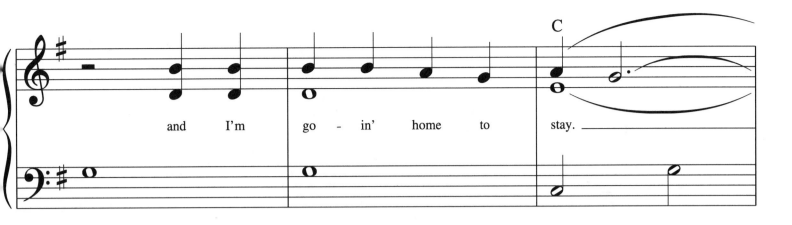

and I'm go - in' home to stay. _____

_____ I'm go - in' _____

G/D   D   Dsus

home   for   Christ - mas _____ and noth - in's gon - na

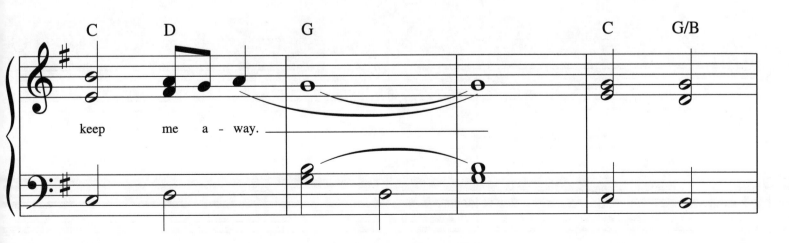

C   D   G   C   G/B

keep me a - way. _____

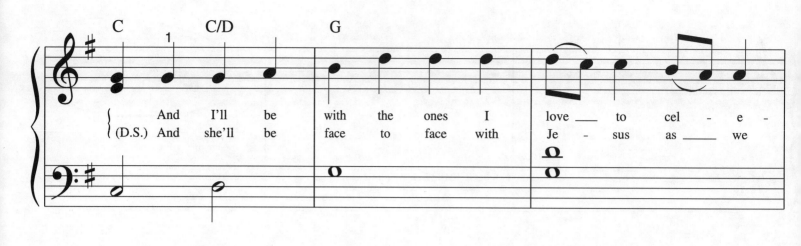

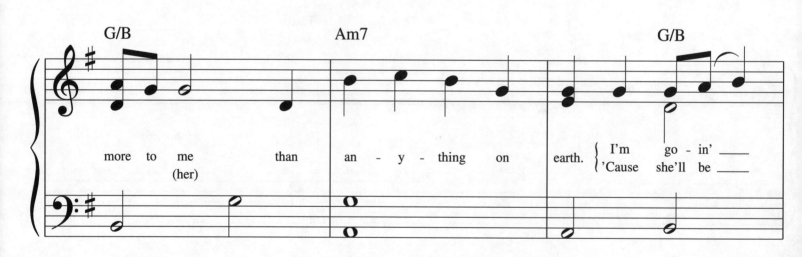

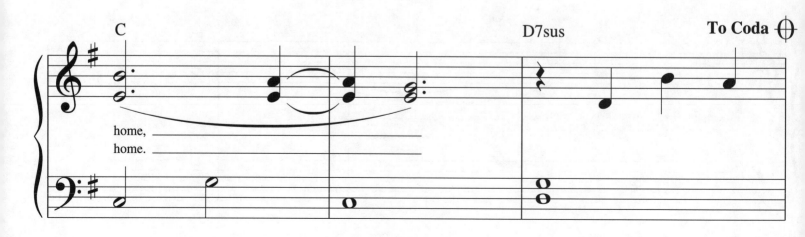

22

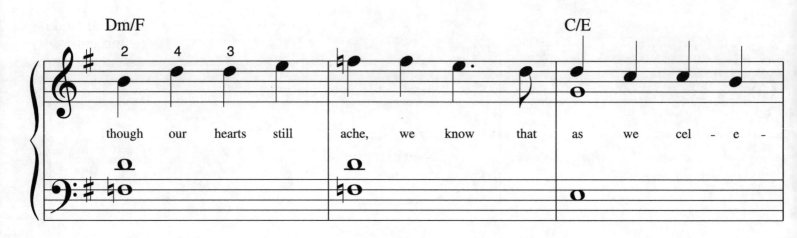

though our hearts still ache, we know that as we cel - e -

brate, she's sing - in' with the her - ald an - gels and heav - en's

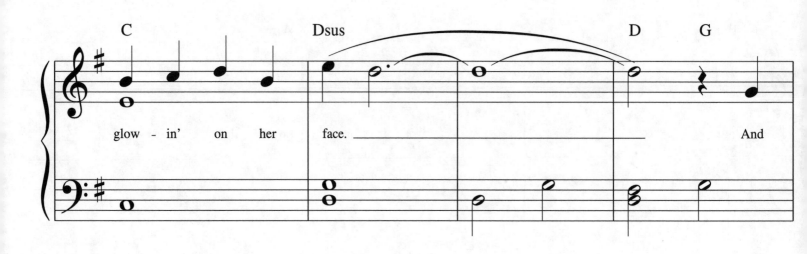

glow - in' on her face. _____ And

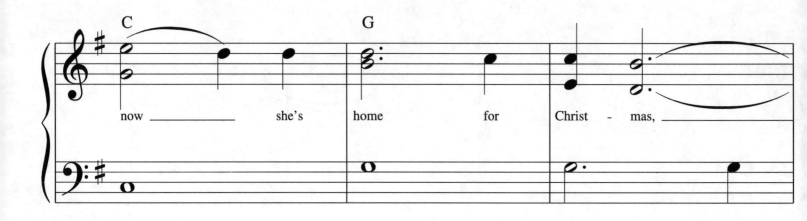

now _____ she's home for Christ - mas, _____

_____ oh, _____ now she's home to stay. _____

Oh, she's home _____ for

Christ - mas; noth - ing could - 've kept her _____ a -

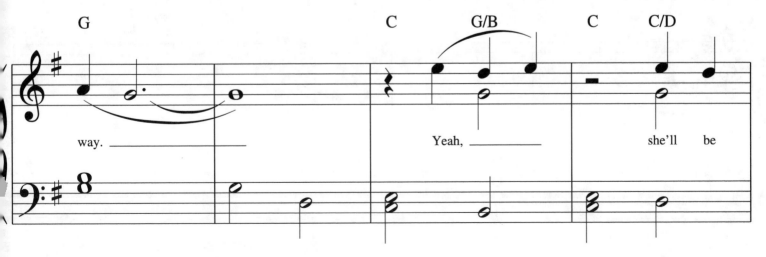

way. _____ Yeah, _____ she'll be

24

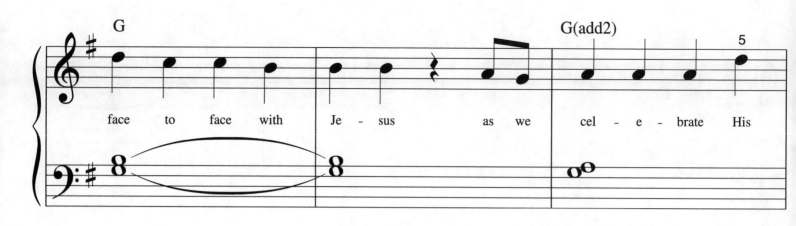

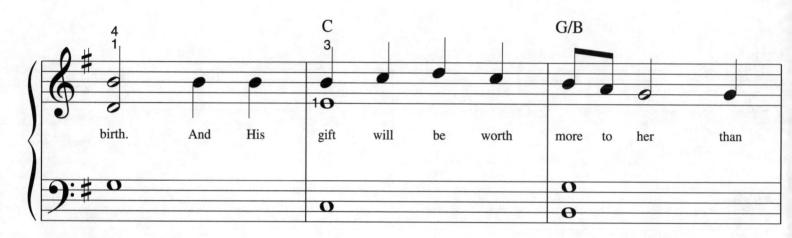

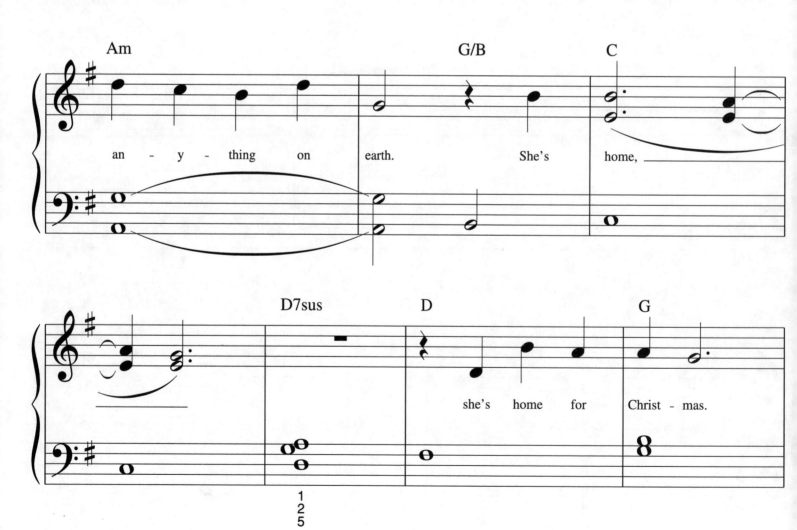

25

And she is home, _____

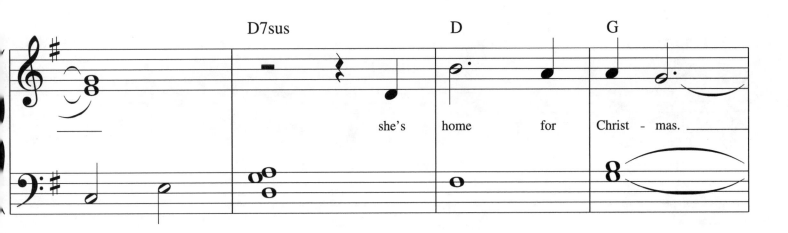

she's home for Christ - mas. _____

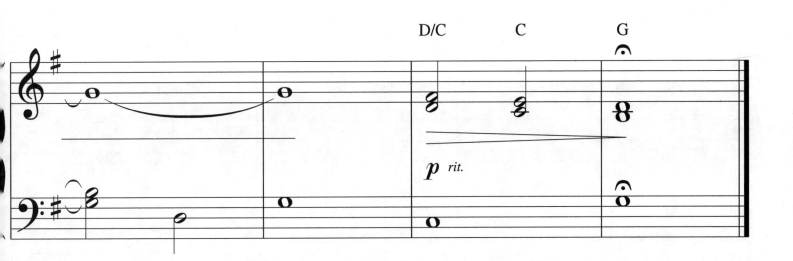

p rit.

Additional Lyrics

3. All the leaves outside have fallen to be covered by the snow.
The fam'ly comes with food and gifts and Grandpa comes alone.
There's a sadness in our silence as the Christmas story's read.
And with tears, Grandpa reminds us of the words that Grandma said.
Chorus

THE CHRISTMAS SHOES

Words and Music by LEONARD AHLSTROM
and EDDIE CARSWELL

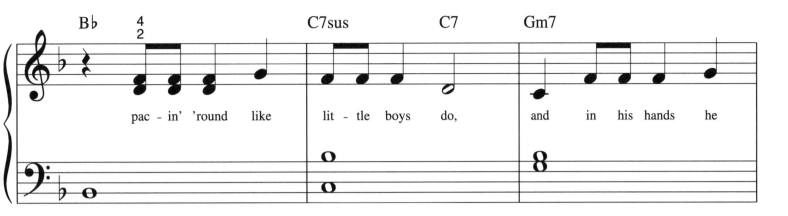

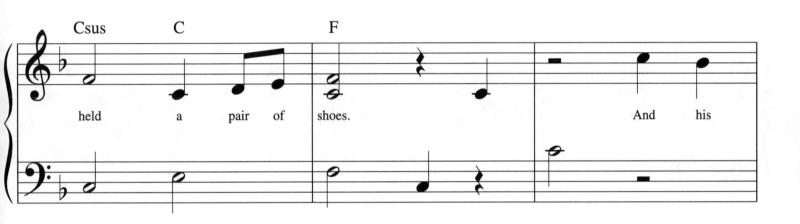

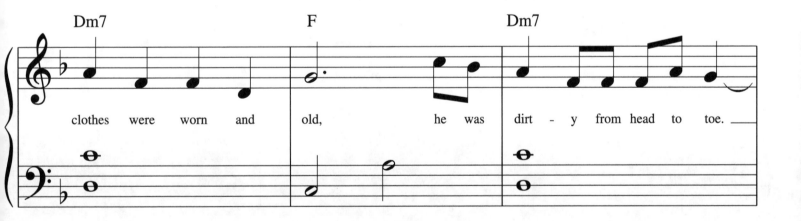

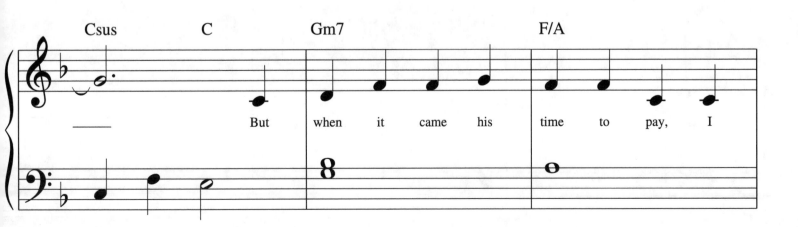

29

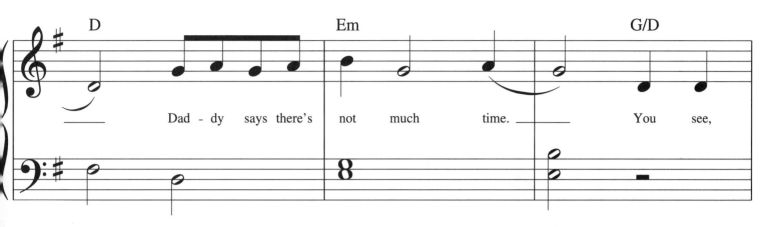

Dad - dy says there's not much time. _____ You see,

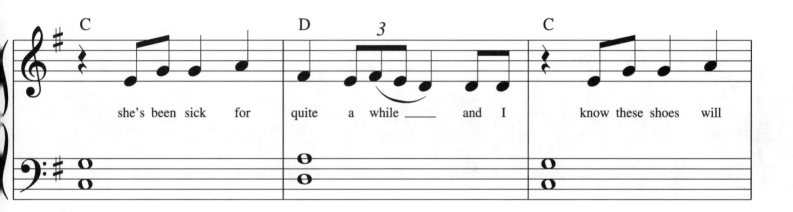

she's been sick for quite a while _____ and I know these shoes will

make her smile _____ and I want her to look beau - ti - ful if

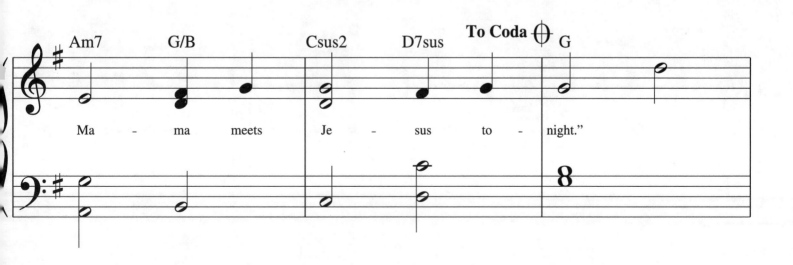

Ma - ma meets Je - sus to - night."

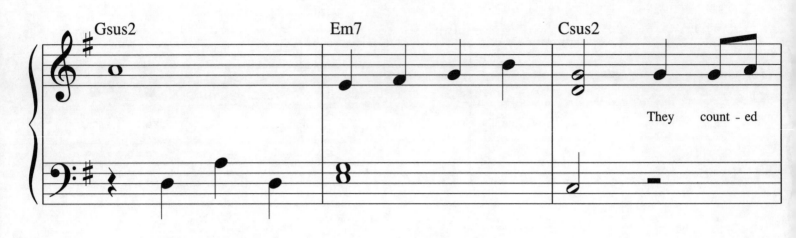

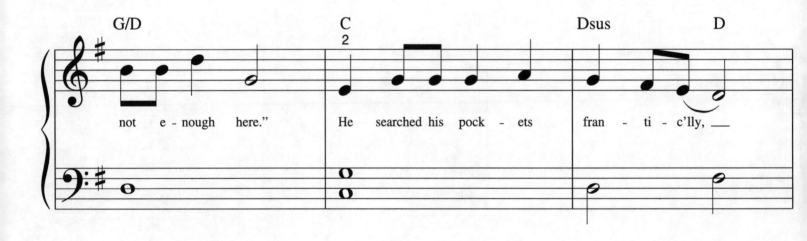

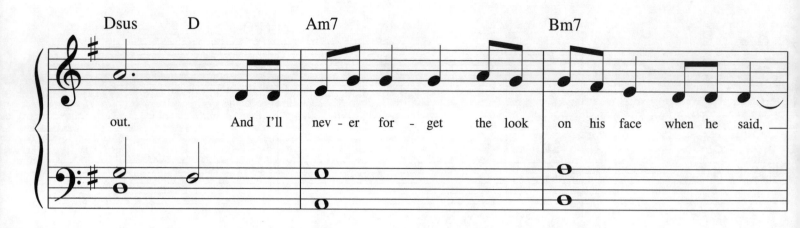

D.S. al Coda

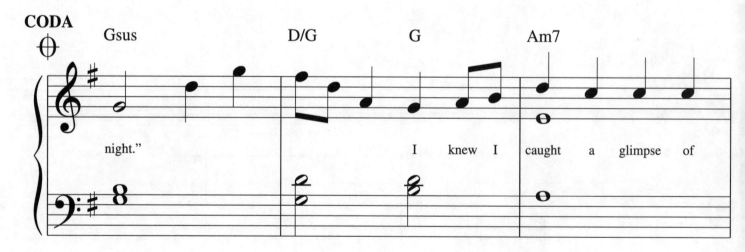

33

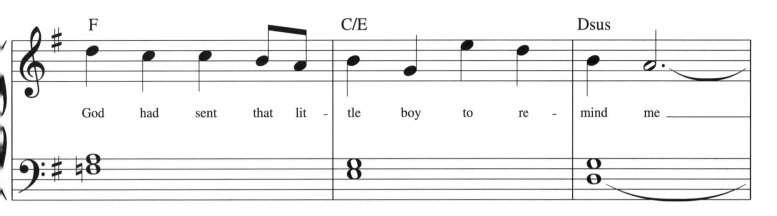

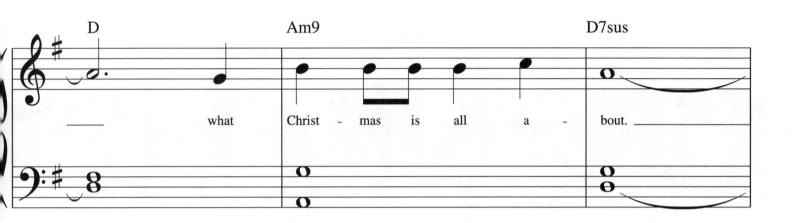

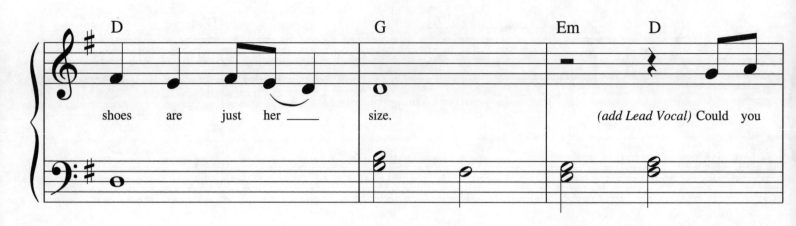

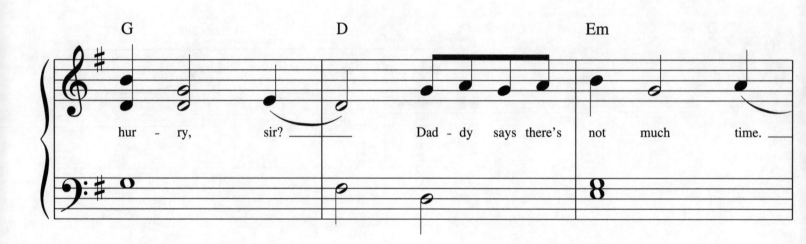

EMMANUEL

Words and Music by
MICHAEL W. SMITH

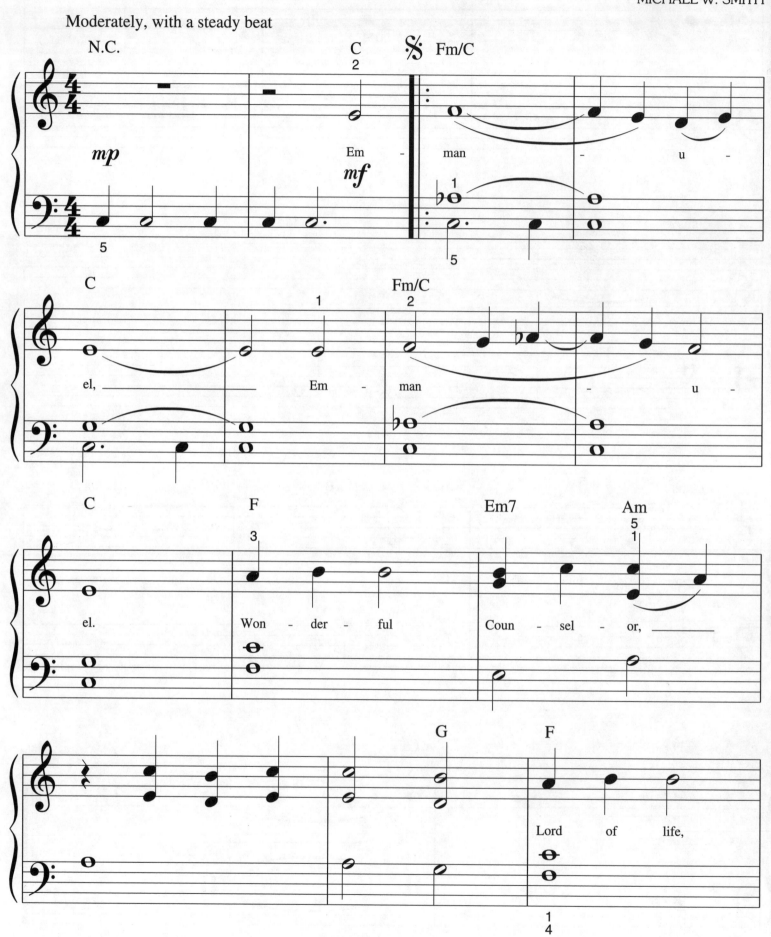

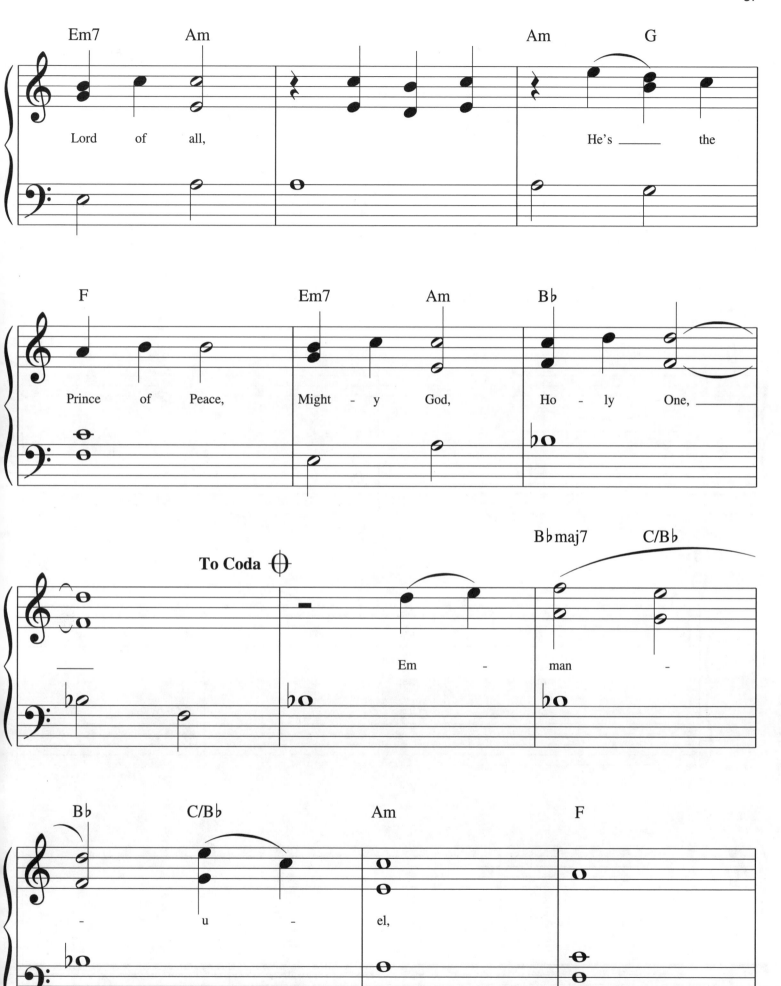

38

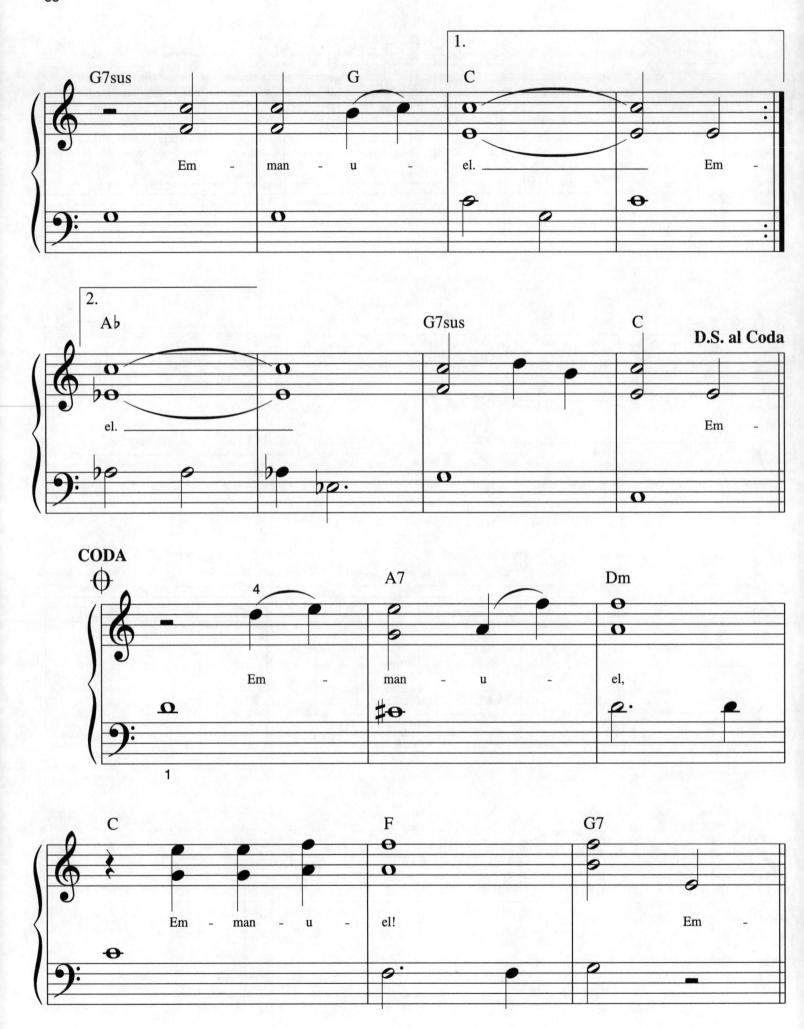

40

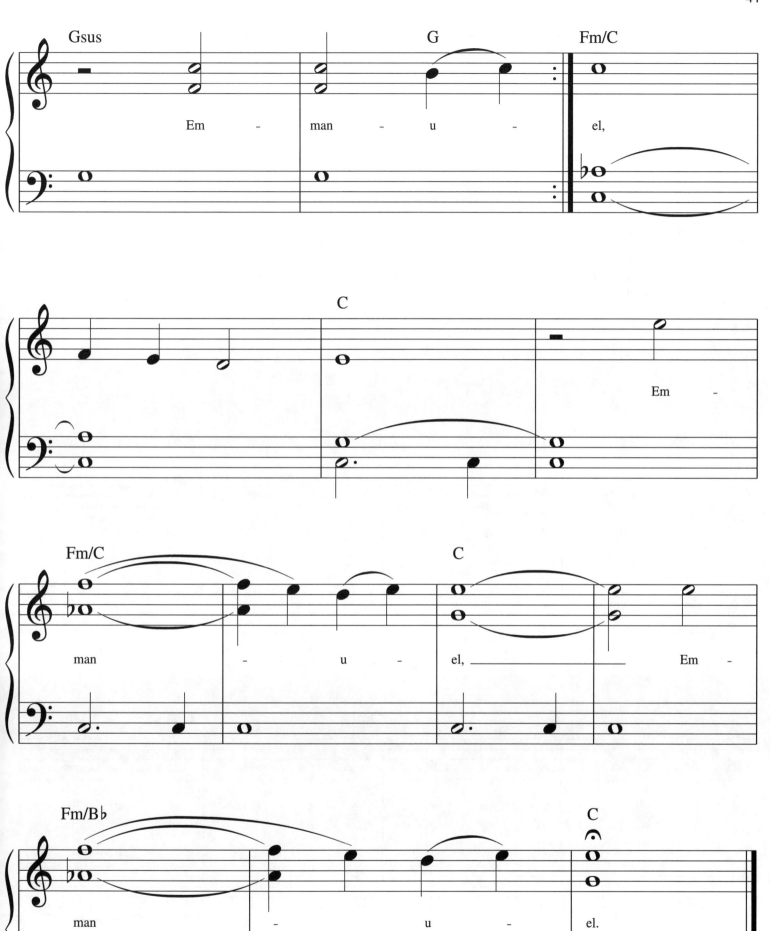

I WONDER AS I WANDER

By JOHN JACOB NILES

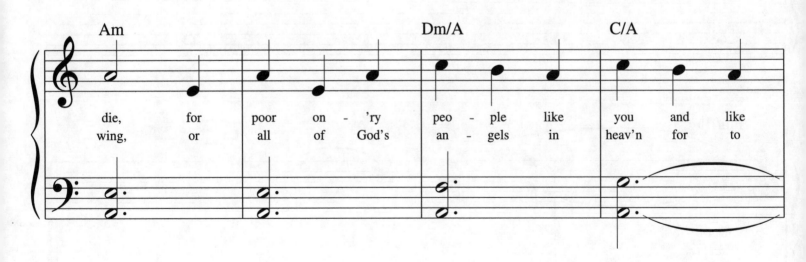

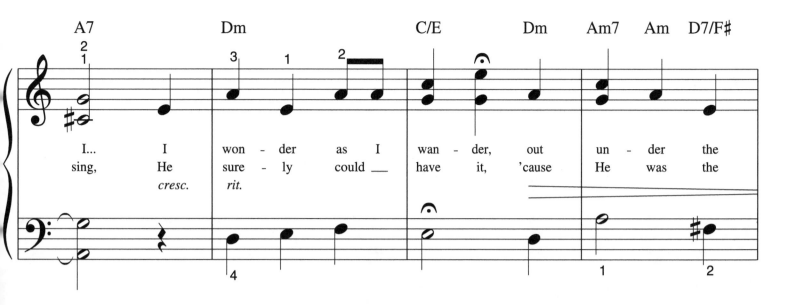

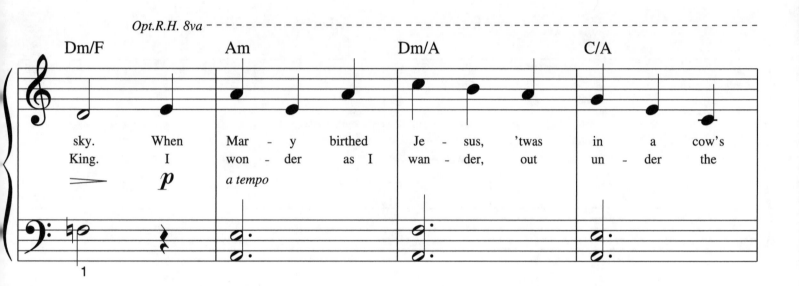

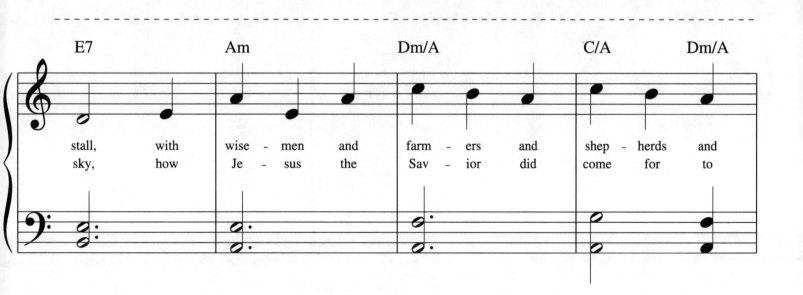

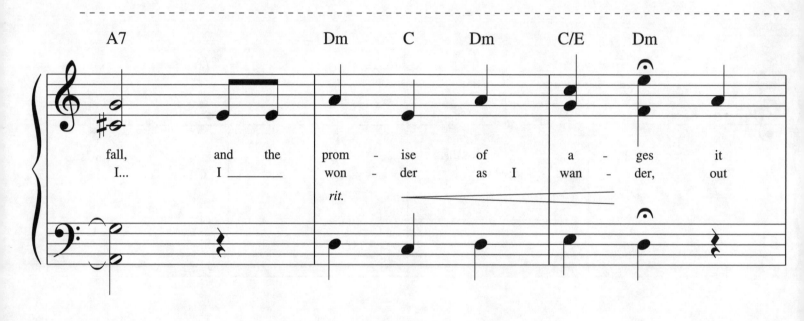

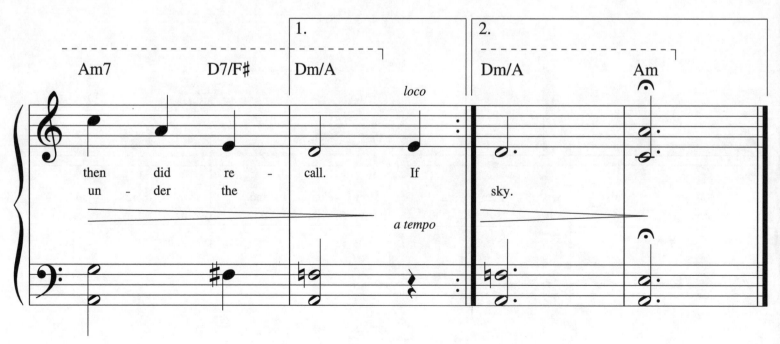

O HOLY NIGHT

French Words by PLACIDE CAPPEAU
English Words by JOHN S. DWIGHT
Music by ADOLPHE ADAM

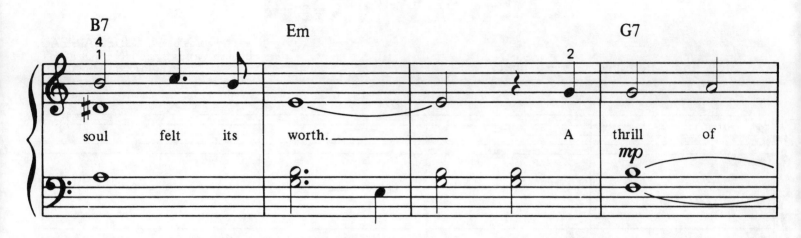

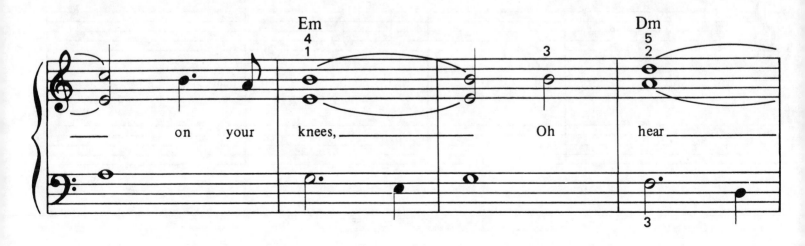

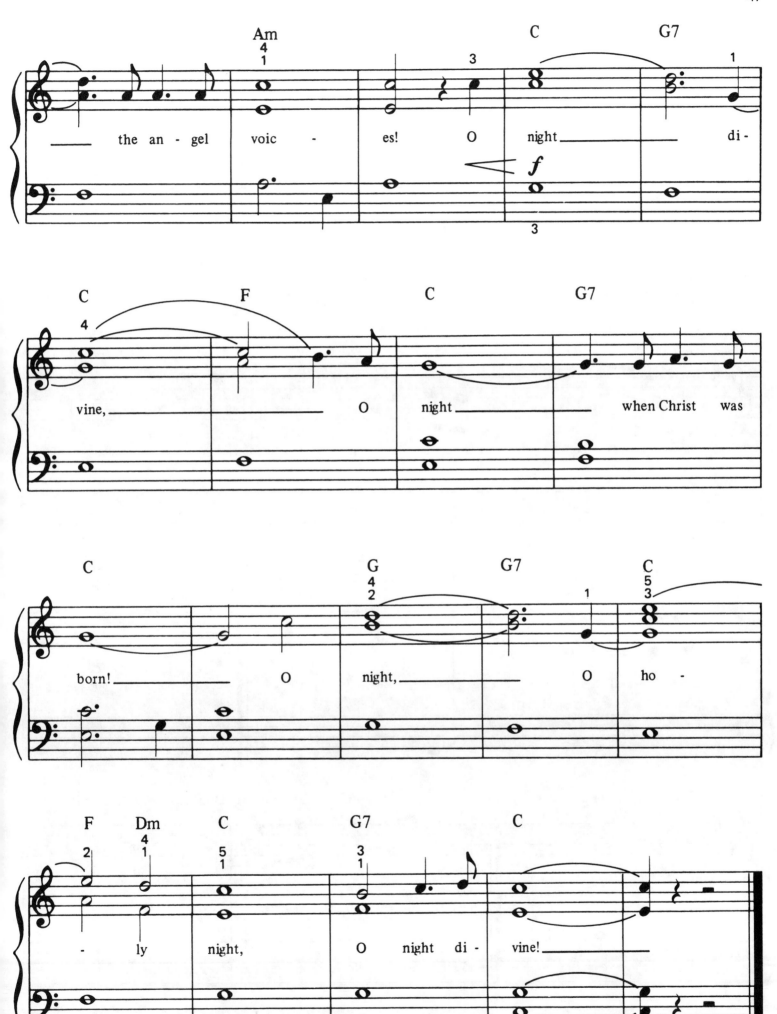

JESUS IS BORN

Words and Music by STEVE GREEN,
PHIL NAISH and COLLEEN GREEN

50

51

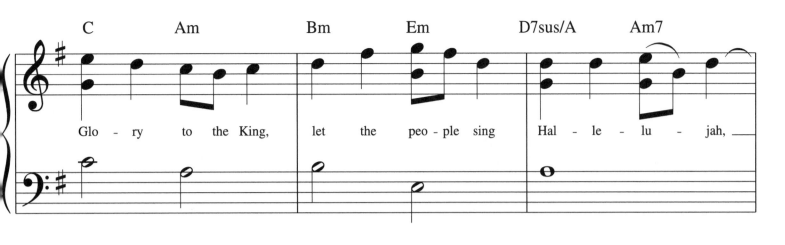

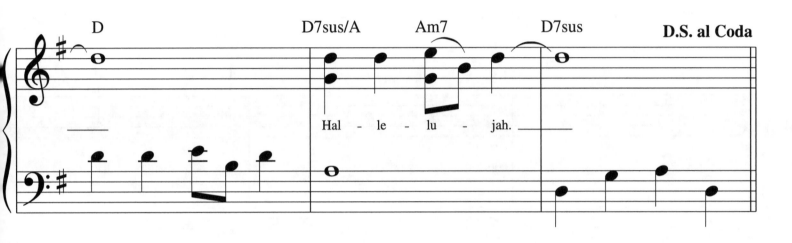

CODA

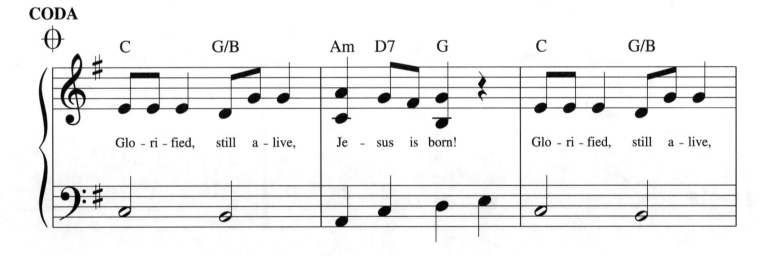

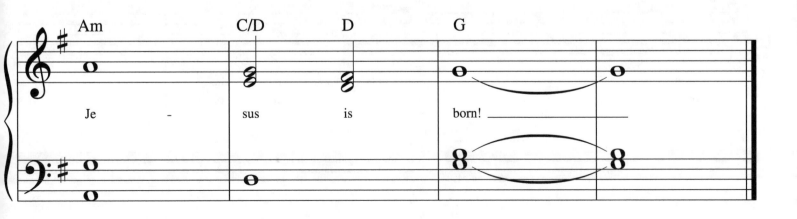

PRECIOUS PROMISE

Words and Music by
STEVEN CURTIS CHAPMAN

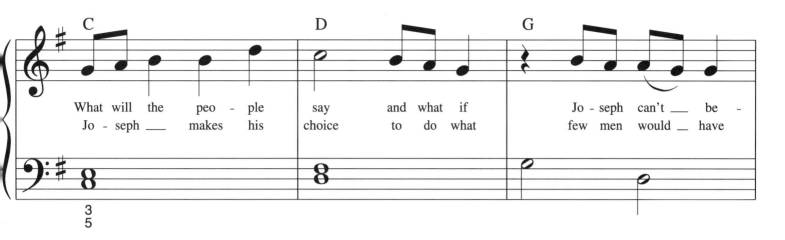

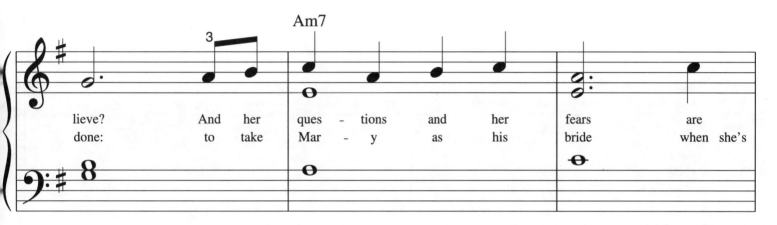

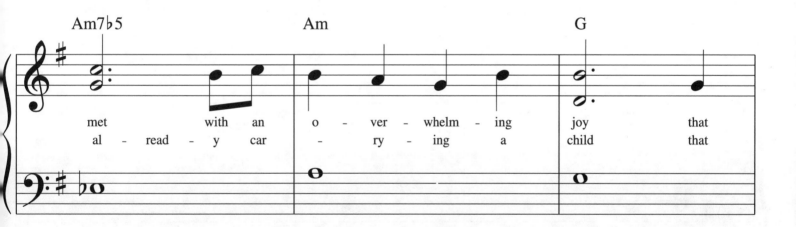

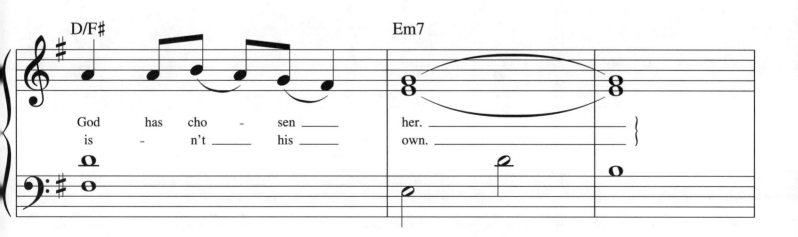

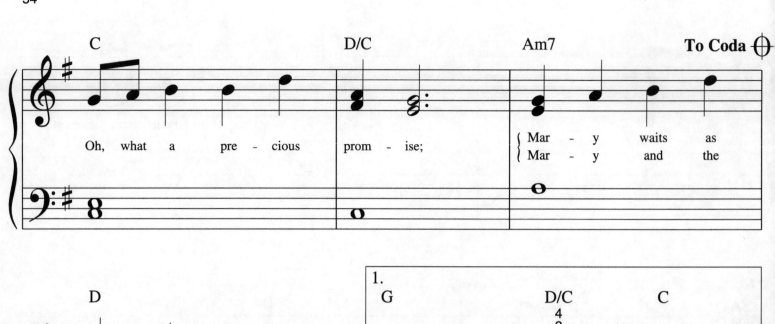

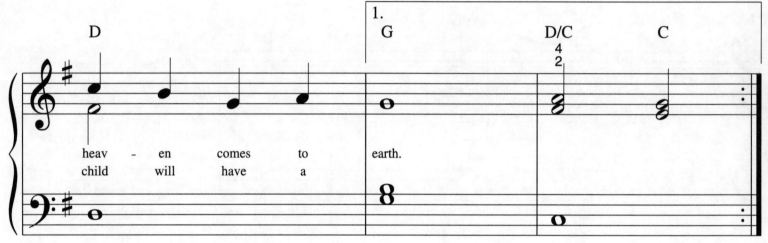

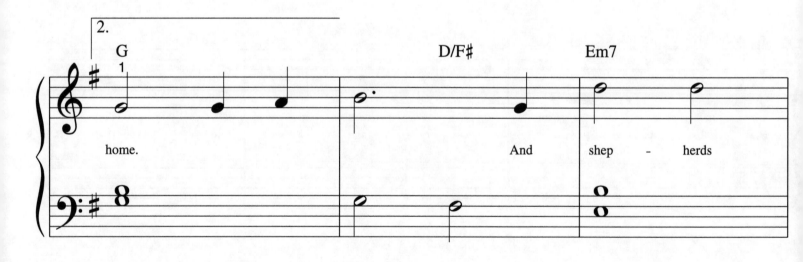

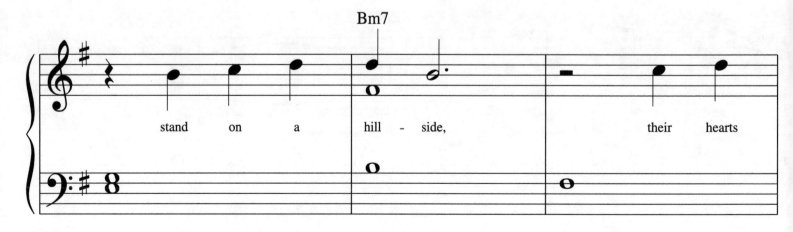

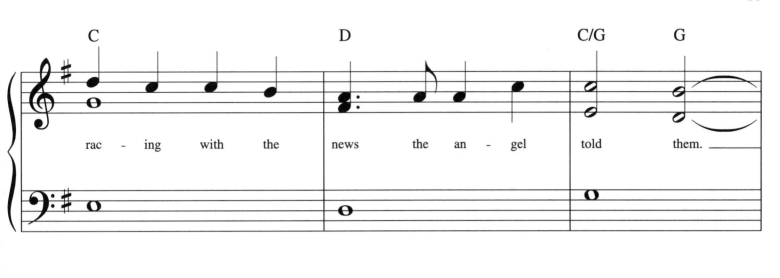

rac - ing with the news the an - gel told them. _____

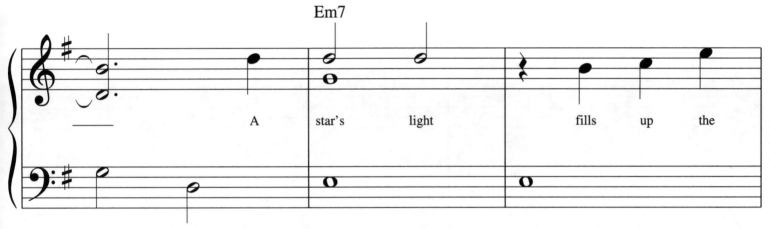

_____ A star's light fills up the

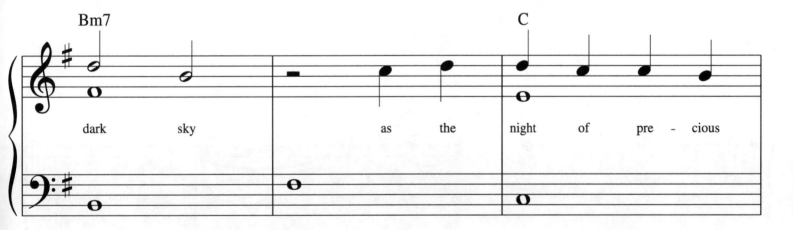

dark sky as the night of pre - cious

prom - ise is un - fold - ing. _____

D.S. al Coda

CODA

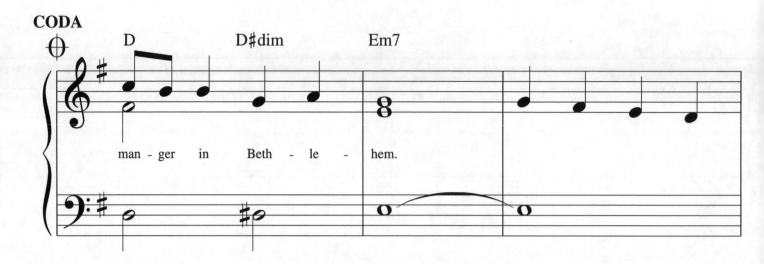

man - ger in Beth - le - hem.

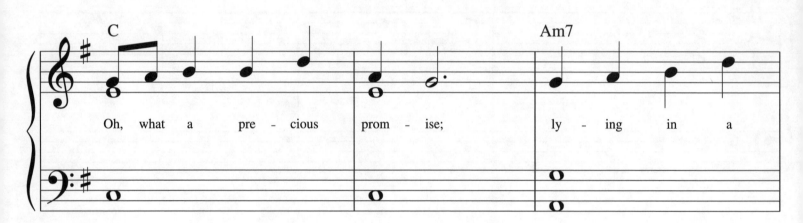

Oh, what a pre - cious prom - ise; ly - ing in a

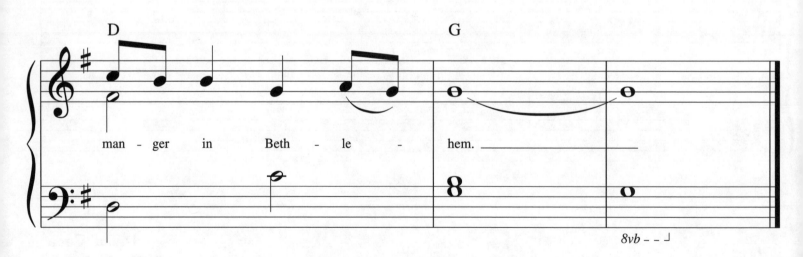

man - ger in Beth - le - hem. _____

8vb - - ⌐

Additional Lyrics

3. Oh, what a precious promise, oh, what a gift of love.
   The waiting now is over and the time has fin'lly come
   For the God who made this world to roll back the curtain
   And unveil His passion for the heart of man,
   Oh, what a precious promise; lying in a manger in Bethlehem.
   Oh, what a precious promise; lying in a manger in Bethlehem.

ROSE OF BETHLEHEM

Words and Music by
LOWELL ALEXANDER

SOME CHILDREN SEE HIM

Lyric by WIHLA HUTSON
Music by ALFRED BURT

1. Some

chil - dren see Him li - ly ___ white, The Ba - by Je - sus ___ born this night. Some
2. chil - dren see Him al - mond - eyed, This Sav - ior whom we ___ kneel be - side, Some
3. *(See additional lyrics)*

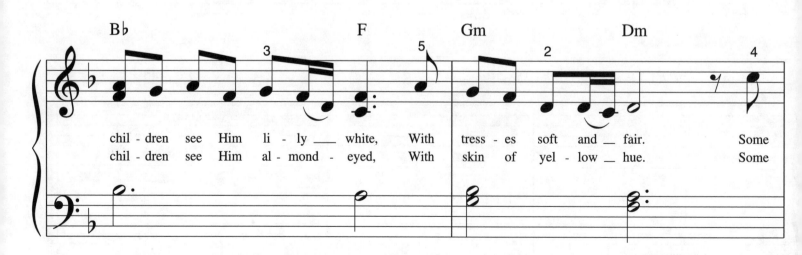

chil - dren see Him li - ly ___ white, With tress - es soft and ___ fair. Some
chil - dren see Him al - mond - eyed, With skin of yel - low ___ hue. Some

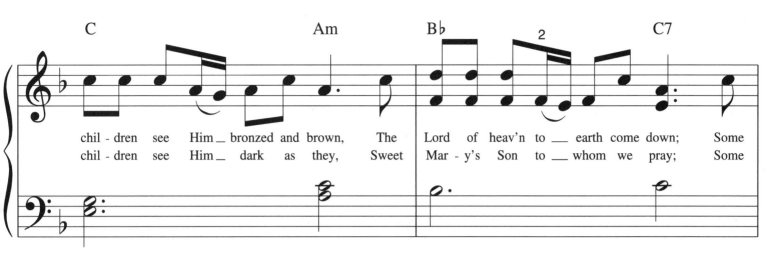

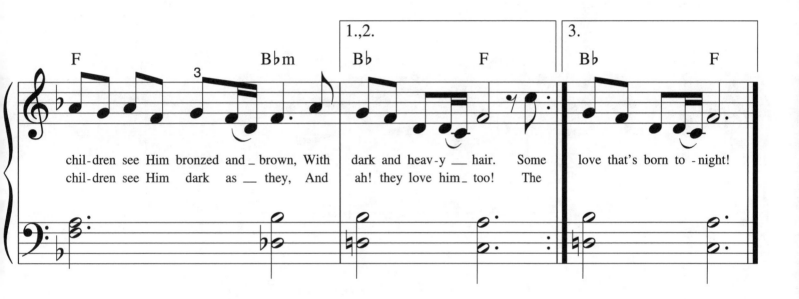

Additional Lyrics

3. The children in each diff'rent place
   Will see the Baby Jesus' face
   Like theirs, but bright with heav'nly grace,
   And filled with holy light.

   O lay aside each earthly thing,
   And with thy heart as offering,
   Come worship now the Infant King,
   'Tis love that's born tonight!

THE STAR CAROL

Lyric by WIHLA HUTSON
Music by ALFRED BURT

THIS BABY

Words and Music by
STEVEN CURTIS CHAPMAN

66

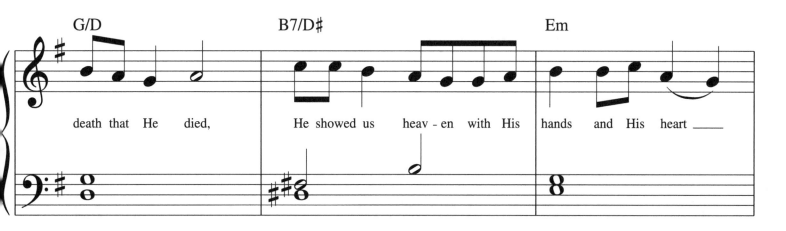

G/D ... **B7/D♯** ... **Em**

death that He died, | He showed us heav-en with His | hands and His heart ___

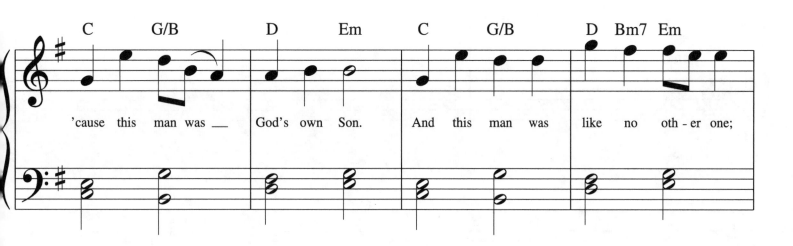

C **G/B** | **D** **Em** | **C** **G/B** | **D** **Bm7** **Em**

'cause this man was ___ | God's own Son. | And this man was | like no oth-er one;

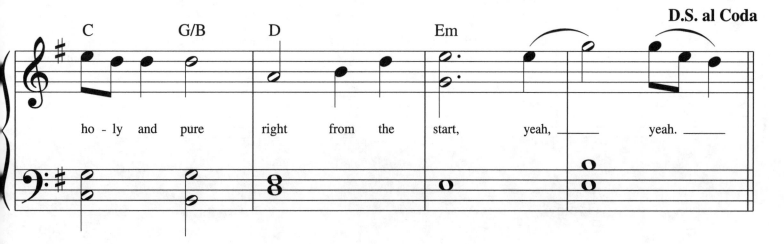

C **G/B** | **D** | **Em**   D.S. al Coda

ho-ly and pure | right from the | start, yeah, ___ yeah. ___

CODA

C | | **G**

This ba-by, | this ba-by was | Je-sus. ___

67

WHO WOULD IMAGINE A KING

from the Touchstone Motion Picture THE PREACHER'S WIFE

Words and Music by MERVYN WARREN
and HALLERIN HILTON HILL

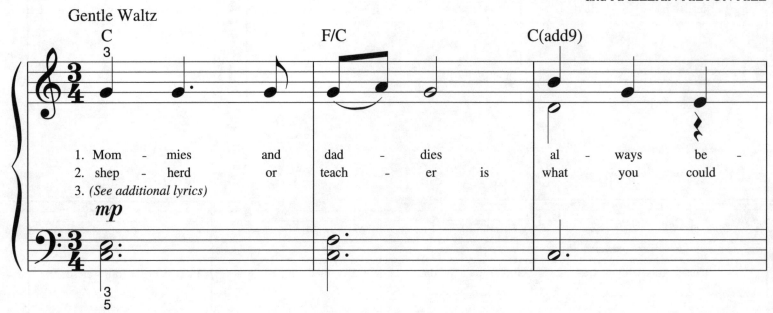

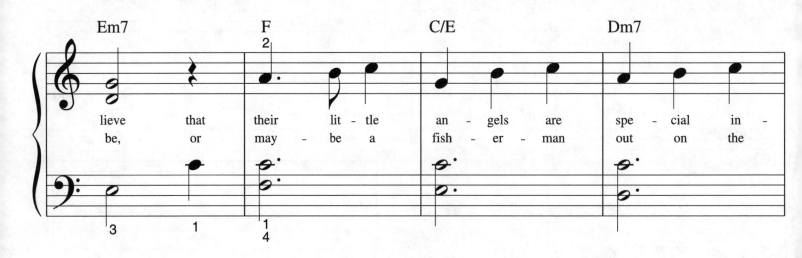

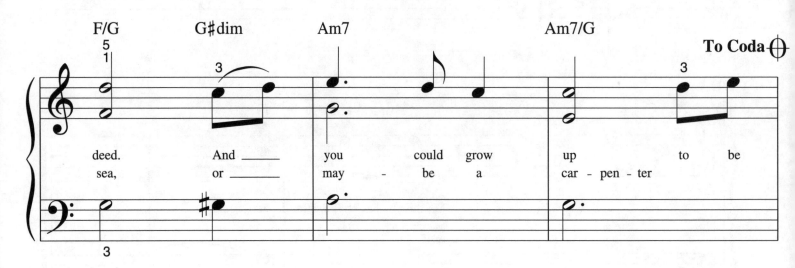

69

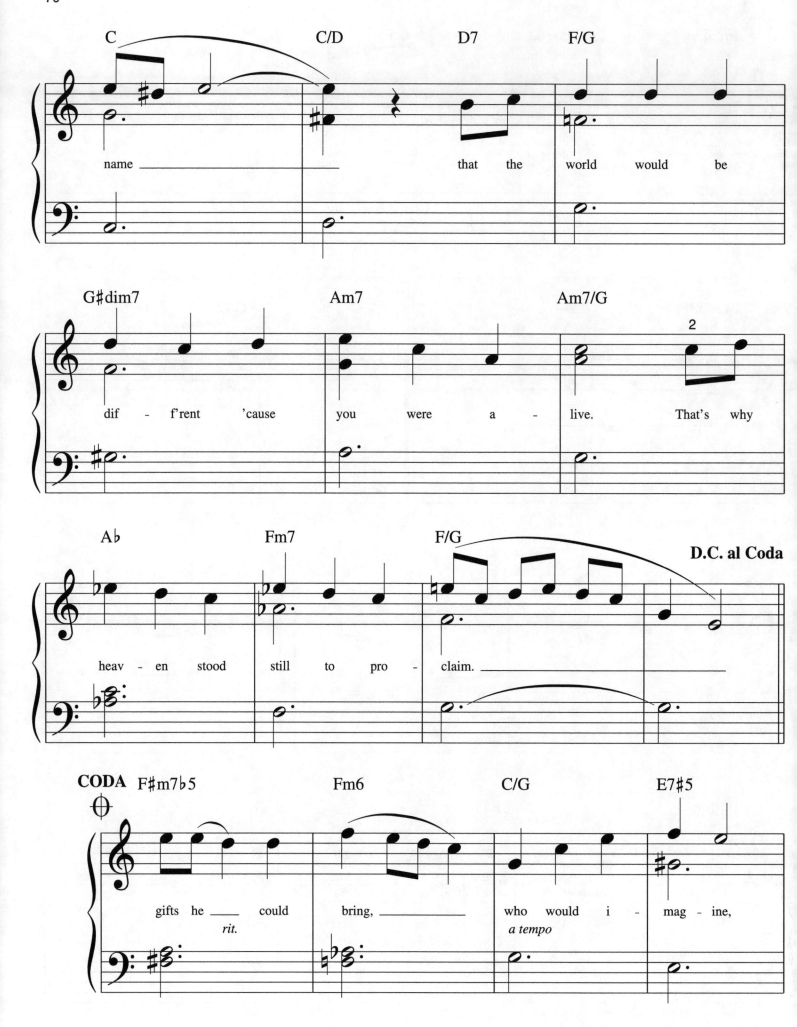

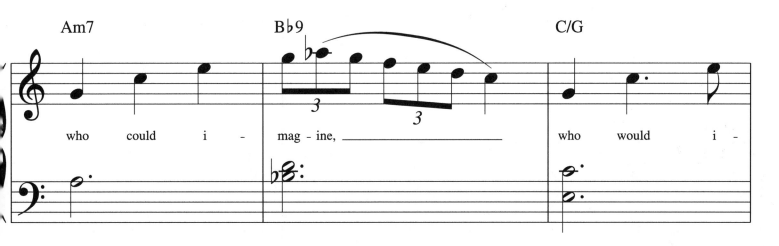

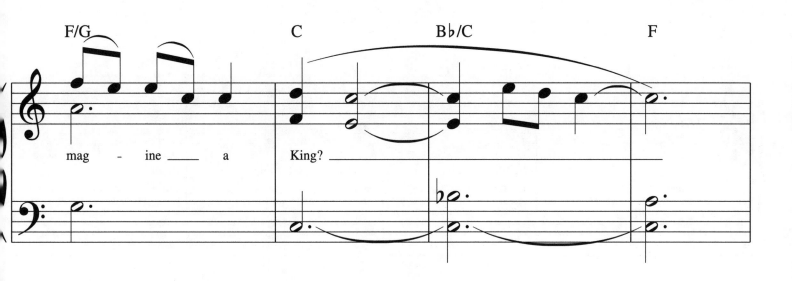

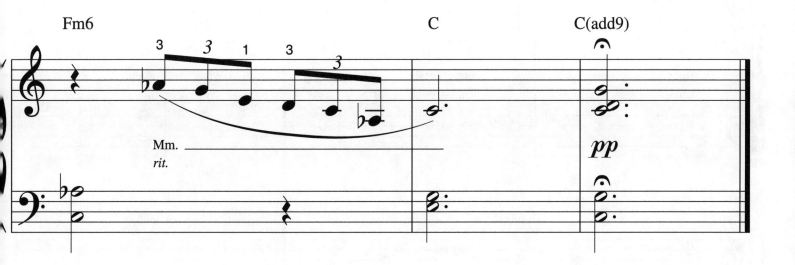

Additional Lyrics

3. One day, an angel said quietly that
   Soon he would bring something special to me.
   And of all of the wonderful gifts he could bring,
   Who would imagine, who could imagine,
   Who would imagine a King? Mm.

WHAT ARE THE SIGNS

Lyric by BATES G. BURT
Music by ALFRED BURT

Slowly, with reverence